Lasciatemi morire!

Lento — *p dolente* — Claudio Monteverdi

La - scia - te - mi mo - ri - re! la - scia - te - no
No long - er let me lan - guish! no long - er

Se Florindo è fedele

Allegretto grazioso, moderato assai — Alessandro Scarlatti

Se Flo - rin - do è fe - de - le io m'in - na -
Should Flo - rin - do be faith - ful Sure - ly I'll

Vergin, tutto amor

Largo religioso — Francesco Durante

Ver - gin, tut - to a - mor, o ma - dre di bon -
Vir - gin, fount of love, Dear Moth - er, thou of

Die Alte

Ein bischen durch die Nase. — W.A. Mozart

1. Zu mei - ner Zeit, zu mei - ner Zeit be - stand noch Recht und

Wiegenlied.

Zart bewegt. — Johannes Brahms

Gu - ten A - bend, gut' Nacht, mit Ro - sen be - dacht, mit

Es hat die Rose sich beklagt

Larghetto — Fervent and tender. (*Innig und zart*) — Robert Franz

The rose com - plain'd with hang - ing head Her fragrance
Es hat die Ro se sich be klagt das gar zu

THE VIRGIN'S SLUMBER SONG

Allegretto — *p* — MAX REGER

A - mid the ros - es Ma - ry sits and rocks her Je - sus - child,
Ma - ri - a sitzt am Ro - sen - hag und wiegt ihr Je - sus - kind,

Sweet Little Jesus Boy

With simplicity and sincerity, *Slowly* — Robert MacGimsey

Sweet lit - tle Je - sus Boy they,

Ride On, King Jesus!

Maestoso — Spiritual arr. H. T. Burleigh

Ride on, King Je - sus! No man can - a

2

PERFORMANCE GUIDE
COMMENTARY BY CARLINE RAY

CLAUDIO MONTEVERDI
Lasciatemi Morire!

"Lasciateme Morire" is the sole surviving piece from the opera *Arianna* of 1608. It is best known in the 5-part madrigal form into which it was later arranged, but in its original form, it is a perfect example of the *seconda prattica,* or monodic style. The mood of the song is grieving and anguished, requiring highly controlled intensity. Allow the dynamic levels to work for you, and notice the melodic depiction of the text. Hold the half notes at the ends of phrases out to their full value. On the last word, "morire," let the tone die away slowly, but do not let it get breathy.

ALESSANDRO SCARLATTI
Se Florindo è Fedele

This song is characterized by a very intriguing rhythmic pattern, with pairs of 3-bar phrases separated by one measure which anticipates the repetition. Also note the imitation between the piano and the voice. The feeling throughout is light and carefree, but the tempo is moderate, not a true allegro. In the phrase "io m'innamorero" at the beginning of the song, keep the grace note light and quick, putting the accent on the sixteenth note which follows on the beat.

FRANCESCO DURANTE
Vergin, Tutto Amor

"Vergin, Tutto Amor" is a prayer to the Virgin Mary, a plea for her to listen to a sinner and have mercy. Control your breathing carefully and sing the phrases in long, legato lines whenever possible. For dramatic effect, you may take a quick breath between the first two "pietosos" that occur in measures 16 and 17; then on the third "pietoso" carry the phrase out to the end of the sentence. Keep the prayerful mood without becoming over-emotional.

WOLFGANG A. MOZART
Die Alte

One of Mozart's relatively few songs, "Die Alte" is typically short and simple. It should be performed in a very speech-like, non-legato manner. Exaggerate the pronounciation of the words, which explain how things were "in my time." The composer instructs the singer to sing a little through the nose.

JOHANNES BRAHMS
Wiegenlied

This most famous of lullabies is also one of the most unusual — the piano accompaniment is based on a traditional Austrian landler, or dance song. This accompaniment effectively represents a gently rocking cradle. It will take considerable control to sing the *Wiegenlied* softly, yet with focused tones and intelligible words. In the phrase "morgen fruh, wenn Gott will," do not let the upper octave note on "fruh" become any louder than the lower octave notes on "morgen." Make this a true lullaby; caress the words and lull the baby to sleep.

ROBERT FRANZ
Es Hat Die Rose Sich Beklagt

This song is a complaint by a rose that all too soon her perfume fades, to which the poet gives assurance to her that through his songs her sweetness will be eternal. Sing with expressive tenderness, never letting the dynamic level reach higher than mezzo forte. At the end of each phrase are two eighth notes; lighten up on the second of these to make a "feminine" ending.

MAX REGER
The Virgin's Slumber Song

This lovely lullaby describes the Virgin Mother rocking her baby to sleep as the soft, warm breezes blow through the trees. The melody itself is simple, but it is nevertheless difficult to maintain a legato line while negotiating skips of thirds, fourths, and fifths. Again, never rise above *piano.* Note especially the marking of pianissimo on the phrase "Ah, baby, dear one;" the top note on the word "Ah" should be the softest note of the phrase.

ROBERT MacGIMSEY
Sweet Little Jesus Boy

This is yet another version of a lullaby sung to the Jesus Child. The composer gives very explicit instructions for its performance: "Never hurry the words. Dwell on the meaningful words here and there according to your own feelings . . . Bear in mind that this is a meditative song of suppressed emotion, sung by you intimately to the Jesus Child."

SPIRITUAL (arr. Burleigh)
Ride On, King Jesus!

This spiritual has a majestic, deeply religious conviction that sorrow will turn to joy, that all things that oppress the soul will soon be lifted, and that every man will be free. Keep these ideas in mind when singing this well-known song.

Carline Ray

Lasciatemi morire!
No longer let me languish
Canto from the opera "Arianna"

English version by
Dr. Theodore Baker

Claudio Monteverdi

Se Florindo è fedele

Should Florindo be faithful

Arietta

English version by
Dr. Theodore Baker

Alessandro Scarlatti

18

more - re - rò, s'è fe - de - le Flo - rin - do m'in -
fall in love, Should Flo - rin - do be faith - ful I'll

cresc.

f

22

dolce

na - mo - re - rò, io m'in - na - mo - re - rò, s'è fe -
sure-ly fall in love, I'll sure - ly fall in love; If Flo -

p

p

27

f

p

de - le Flo - rin - do m'in - na - mo - re - rò,
rin - do be faith - ful I'll sure-ly fall in love,

f

p

p

31

rall.

m'in - na - mo - re - rò, m'in - na - mo - re - rò,
I shall fall in love, I shall fall in love,

col canto

imitando la voce

io m'in - na - mo - re - rò.
I'll sure-ly, sure-ly fall in love.

Po - tra ben l'ar-co ten - de - re il fa - re -
How art - ful e'er he draw the bow, Well - vers'd in__

tra-to ar - cier, ch'io mi sa-prò di - fen - de - re d'un
arch-ers' wiles, My heart I can de - fend, I know, From

guar - do lu - sin - ghier. Pre - ghi,
an - y lur - ing smiles. Sigh-ing,

55
pian - ti e que - re - le, io non a-scol - te - rò,
weep-ing, and im-plor-ing, My breast can nev - er move:

60
con grazioso
ma se sa - rà fe - de - le, ma se sa - rà fe - de - le io
But if he should be faith-ful, but if he should be faith - ful I'll

64
m'in - na - mo - re - rò, io m'in - na - mo - re
sure-ly fall in love, I'll sure-ly fall in

68
rall.
rò, m'in - na - mo - re - rò, m'in - na - mo - re
love, I shall fall in love, I shall fall in

col canto   imitando il canto

Vergin, tutto amor
Virgin, fount of love
Preghiera
Prayer

English version by
Dr. Theodore Baker

Francesco Durante

Die Alte

(Friedrich von Hagedorn.)

(Orig. Emoll.)

W.A. Mozart

3 taps (1 and 1/2 bars) precede music.

Ein bischen durch die Nase.

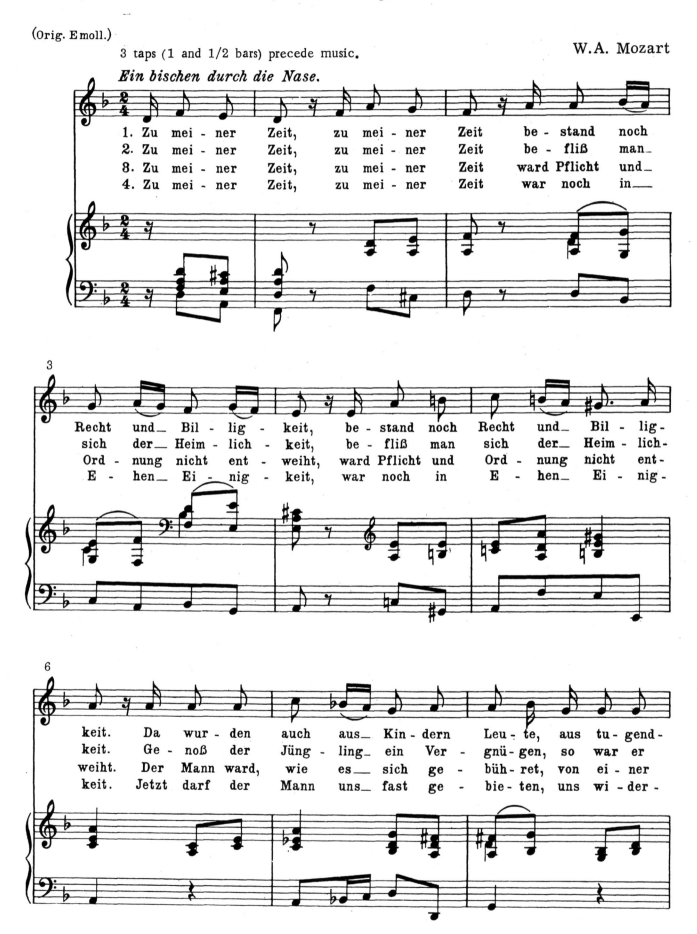

1. Zu mei - ner Zeit, zu mei - ner Zeit be - stand noch Recht und Bil - lig - keit, be - stand noch Recht und Bil - lig - keit. Da wur - den auch aus Kin - dern Leu - te, aus tu - gend-

2. Zu mei - ner Zeit, zu mei - ner Zeit be - fliß man sich der Heim - lich - keit, be - fliß man sich der Heim - lich - keit. Ge - noß der Jüng - ling ein Ver - gnü - gen, so war er

8. Zu mei - ner Zeit, zu mei - ner Zeit ward Pflicht und Ord - nung nicht ent - weiht, ward Pflicht und Ord - nung nicht ent - weiht. Der Mann ward, wie es sich ge - büh - ret, von ei - ner

4. Zu mei - ner Zeit, zu mei - ner Zeit war noch in E - hen Ei - nig - keit, war noch in E - hen Ei - nig - keit. Jetzt darf der Mann uns fast ge - bie - ten, uns wi - der-

Wiegenlied.

(Orig. Es dur.)

Johannes Brahms
Op. 49. № 4.

Zart bewegt.

Teneramente, con moto.

Gu-ten A - bend, gut' Nacht, mit Ro - sen be - dacht, mit Näg'-lein be - steckt, schlupf' un - ter die Deck': mor-gen früh, wenn Gott will, wirst du wie - der ge - weckt, mor-gen früh, wenn Gott will, wirst du wie - der ge - weckt.

THE ROSE COMPLAINED
(Es hat die Rose sich beklagt)

FRIEDRICH von BODENSTEDT
(From the Persian of Mirza Schaffy)
Translated by George L. Osgood

ROBERT FRANZ, Op.42, No 5

THE VIRGIN'S SLUMBER SONG
(MARIÄ WIEGENLIED)

From the collection of "Simple Melodies" by Max Reger

MARTIN BOELITZ
English version by Ed. Teschemacher

(Original Key, F)

MAX REGER, Op. 76, № 52

Sweet Little Jesus Boy

Words and Music by
ROBERT Mac GIMSEY

Sing this song with the simplicity of a lullaby to a child.
Never hurry the words. Dwell on the meaningful words here
and there according to your own feelings, and maintain no
rhythm whatsoever.

Bear in mind that this is a meditative song of suppressed emotion, sung by you intimately to the Jesus Child.

CODA
(Under the breath, as though talking to one's self)

Sweet lit - tle Je - sus Boy __ born long time a - go __
(bawn)

Sweet lit - tle Ho - ly Child __ And we did - n't know who you were.
(Chil') __ (An') (wus)

Ride On, King Jesus!

Ps. 45, 4
Rev. 6, 2

Negro Spiritual
Arranged by
H. T. BURLEIGH

MMO 7001 Schubert: Songs for High Voice, vol. 1
MMO 7002 Schubert: Songs for Low Voice, vol. 1

An die Musik — Die Forelle* — Auf dem Wasser zu singen — Du bist die Ruh — Wohin? — Nacht und Träume — Ständchen — Heidenröslein — Gretchen am Spinnrade — Erlkönig** — Der Musensohn* — Romanze aus "Rosamunde" — Aufenthalt** — Lachen und Weinen* — Der Tod und das Mädchen — An Silvia — Seligkeit — *high voice only **low voice only.

MMO 7003 Schubert: Songs for High Voice, vol. 2
MMO 7004 Schubert: Songs for Low Voice, vol. 2

Frühlingsglaube — Im Frühling — Dass sie hier gewesen — Die Liebe hat gelogen — Du liebst mich nicht — Erster Verlust — Die Allmacht — Ganymed — Wanderers Nachtlied — Nahe des Geliebten — Rastlose Liebe — Fischerweise — Im Abendrot — Ungeduld Nachtviolen —

MMO 7005 Brahms: Songs for High Voice
MMO 7006 Brahms: Songs for Low Voice

Die Mainacht — An die Nachtigall — Alte Liebe** — Bei dir sind meine Gedanken* — Botschaft — Immer leiser wird mein Schlummer — Liebestreu — Von ewiger Liebe — Dein blaues Auge** — Meine Liebe ist grun — O wusst' ich doch den Weg — Sonntag — Ständchen* — Der Tod, das ist die kuhle Nacht* — Vergebliches Ständchen — Wie Melodien zieht es mir — Auf dem Kirchhofe** — Sapphische Ode** — *high voice **low voice

MMO 7007 Everybody's Favorites for High Voice, vol. 1
MMO 7008 Everybody's Favorites for Low Voice, vol. 1

Songs My Mother Taught Me — None but the lonely heart — I Love Thee — Ave Maria (Schubert—Bach-Gounod) — Si mes vers avaient des ailes — Wiegenlied — Last Rose of Summer — Dedication — Apres un reve — Now sleeps the crimson petal — Drink to me only with thine eyes — Tu lo sai — My heart ever faithful — My Mother bids me bind my hair —

MMO 7009 Everybody's Favorites for High Voice, vol. 2
MMO 7010 Everybody's Favorites for Low Voice, vol. 2

Das Veilchen — Die Lotosblume — Ich Liebe dich (Beethoven) — Tu lo sai — Music for a while — Where'er you walk — Der Nussbaum — On Wings of Song — Londonderry Air — Greensleeves — Believe me, if all those endearing young charms — Beau Soir — Verborgenheit — Still wie die Nacht — Litanei — Zueignung —

MMO 7011 17th & 18th Century Italian Songs for High Voice, vol. 1
MMO 7012 17th & 18th Century Italian Songs for Low Voice, vol. 1

Selve amiche — Vittoria. mio cuore — Lasciatemi morire — Gia il sole dal Gange — Udite, amanti — Sospiri di foco — Belle rose purpurine — Bella porta di rubini — Vergin, tutto amor — Caro mio ben — Sfogava con le stelle — Nel puro ardor — Sento nel core —

MMO 7013 17th & 18th Century Italian Songs for High Voice, vol. 2
MMO 7014 17th & 18th Century Italian Songs for Low Voice, vol. 2

Amarilli — Che fiero costume — Danza, danza fanciulla — Occhi immortali — Son ancor pargolette — Ocessate di piagarmi — Se nel ben sempre inconstante — Occhietti amati — Toglietemi la vita ancor — Caldi sospiri — Sonetto spirituale — Sonetto spirituale — Illustratevi, o cieli — Vado ben spesso cangiando loco — Gioite al canto mio —

MMO 7015 Famous Soprano Arias

Ach, ich fuhl's — Deh vieni, non tardar — Mi chiamano Mimi — Un bel di vedremo — Addio, del passato — Ave Maria — Und ob die Wolke — O mio babbino caro — Depuis le jour — Sul fil d'un soffio etesio — Quando m'en vo — Adieu, notre petite table — Jewel Song —

MMO 7016 Famous Mezzo Soprano Arias

Che faro senza Eurydice — Largo — Voi, che sapete — Non so piu cosa son — Connais tu le pays? — Voce di donna — Stride le vampa — Printemps qui commence — Amour, viens aider — Mon coeur s'ouvre a ta voix — Habanera — Seguidilla —

MMO 7017 Famous Tenor Arias

— Dies Bildnis — Dalla sua pace — De' miei bollenti spiriti — La donna e mobile — Aubade — Salut demeure chaste et pure — Le Reve — M'appari — Amor ti vieta — Donna non vidi mai — E lucevan le stelle — Che gelida manina — Flower Song —

MMO 7018 Famous Baritone Arias

Non piu andrai — Deh vieni alla finestra — Der Vogelfanger bin ich ja — Avant de quitter ces lieux (E-Flat) — Avant de quitter ces lieux (D-Flat) — Il balen del suo sorriso — Di Provenza il mar — Toreador Song — Prologue — Alla vita che T'arride — Eri tu che macchiavi — Vision fugitive — O du mein holder Abendstern —

MMO 7019 Famous Bass Arias

O Isis und Osiris — In diesen heil'gen Hallen — Non piu andrai — Vous qui faites l'endormie (Serenade) — Le veau d'or — Vecchia zimarra — Quand'ero paggio — La Calunnia — Vi ravviso, o luoghi ameni — Infelice! e tuo credevi — Ella giammai m'amo — Il lacerato spirito —

MMO 7071 Hugo Wolf Songs for High Voice
MMO 7072 Hugo Wolf Songs for Low Voice

Im Fruhling — Auf ein altes Bild — Gebet — Lebe wohl — In der Fruhe Begegnung* — Auf einer Wanderung** — Der Gartner — Schlafendes Jesuskind — Verschwiegene Liebe* — Nachtzauber — Um Mitternacht** Herr, was tragt der Boden hie — Nun lass uns Frieden schliessen* — Ach, des Knaben Augen — Anakreons Grab — Epiphanias*

MMO 7073 Richard Strauss Songs for High Voice
MMO 7074 Richard Strauss Songs for Low Voice

Heimliche Aufforderung — Allerseelen — Heimkehr — Die Nacht — Morgen Wie Sollten wir — Wiegenlied* — Du meines Herzens Kronelein** — Befreit — Waldseligkeit — Freundliche Vision — Mein Auge* — Icht trage meine Minne** — Traum durch die Dammerung — Standchen Ich schwebe — Cacilie *high voice **low voice

MMO 7075 Sacred Oratorio Arias for Soprano

Alleluia — Et incarnatus — On mighty wings — With verdure clad — Hear ye, Israel — Ich will dir mein herze Schenken — Blute nur — Rejoice greatly — Come unto Him — I know my Redeemer liveth —

MMO 7076 Sacred Oratorio Arias for Alto

O thou that tellest good tidings to Zion — He shall feed His flock — In the battle Prepare thyself, Zion — Keep, O my Spirit — Buss und Reu — Erbarme dich — But the Lord is mindful of His own — Thou shalt bring them in — O rest in the Lord —

MMO 7077 Sacred Oratorio Arias for Tenor

Comfort ye — Every valley — Thou shalt break them — Deposuit — Waft her, angels — In native worth — If with all your hearts — Then shall the righteous — Sound an alarm — Ingemisco —

MMO 7078 Sacred Oratorio Arias for Bass

Now shines the brightest — But who may abide — The trumpet shall sound — Why do the nations? — Honor and arms — Arm, arm ye brave! — Lord, God of Abraham — Is not His word like a fire? — It is enough — Confutatis —

MMO 7101 Schumann Songs for High Voice
MMO 7102 Schumann Songs for Low Voice

Widmung — Du bist wie eine Blume — In der Fremde — Waldesgespräch Mondnacht — Fruhlingsnacht — Der Himmel hat eine Träne geweint — Dein Angesicht — Stille Tränen — Ich grolle nicht Requiem — Aus den hebraischen Gesängen — Meine Rose — Myrten und Rosen — Mein schöner Stern! — Schöne Wiege meiner Leiden.

MMO 7103 Mozart Opera Arias for Soprano

Come Scoglio — In uomini — Una donna a quindici anni (Cosi fan tutte) Non mi dir — Batti, batti — Vedrai carino (Don Giovanni) — Porgi, amor — Dove sono (Marriage of Figaro) — Ach, ich liebte (Abduction).

MMO 7104 Verdi Opera Arias for Soprano

Pace, pace, mio Dio (La Forza) — Ernani, involami (Ernani) — Morrò, ma prima in grazia (Un Ballo) — D'amor sull'ali rosee (Il Trovatore) — Tu che le vanita (Don Carlo) — Oh patria mia (Aida) — Una macchia (Macbeth).

MMO 7105 Italian Opera Arias for Soprano

V'adoro pupille — Piangero (Julius Caesar) — Selva opaca (William Tell) — Donde lieta usci (La Boheme) — Voi lo sapete (Cavelleria) — Io son l'umile ancella — Poveri fiori (Adriana Lecouvreur) — Ebben, n'andrò lontana (La Wally) — L'altra notte (Mefistofele) — Suicidio (La Gioconda).

MMO 7106 French Opera Arias for Soprano

Divinités du Styx (Alceste) — O malheureuse Iphigénie (Sapho) — Pleurez! pleurez mes yeux! (Le Cid) — Air de Lia (L'Enfant Prodigue) — Je dis que rien ne m'epouvante (Carmen) — Il est doux (Herodiade) — Le Roi de Thule (Faust) — O ma lyre immortelle (Sapho).

Soprano Voice Mezzo

Soprano

BEGINNING LEVEL

MMO 9001
KATE HURNEY, soloist
BRUCE EBERLE, pianist
Bononcini/Per la gloria d'adorarvi • Haydn/My Mother Bids Me Bind My Hair • Old Melody/When Love Is Kind • Pergolesi/Stizzoso, mio stizzoso • Purcell/Man Is For The Woman Made • Sullivan/The Moon And I • Weckerlin/Bergère Légère and Jeune Fillette

INTERMEDIATE LEVEL

MMO 9004
KATE HURNEY, soloist
BRUCE EBERLE, pianist
J.S. Bach/My heart ever faithful • Brahms/Vergebliches Standchen • Duke/Loveliest of Trees • Franck/Panis Angelicus • Hahn/Si mes vers avaient des ailes • Mozart/Das Veilchen • Paisiello/Nel cor più non mi sento • Puccini/O Mio Babbino Caro

Mezzo

BEGINNING LEVEL

MMO 9011
FAY KITTELSON, soloist
RICHARD FOSTER, pianist
Barber/The Daisies • Beethoven/Ich liebe dich • Campion/Never Weather-Beaten Sail • Godard/Chanson de Florian • Hopkinson/My Love Is Gone to Sea • Niles/I wonder as I wander • Pergolesi/Se tu m'ami, se sospiri • Scarlatti/O cessate di piagarmi • Schubert/Haiden-Roslein • Thompson/Velvet Shoes

INTERMEDIATE LEVEL

MMO 9014
FAY KITTELSON, soloist
RICHARD FOSTER, pianist
Brahms/Botschaft and Der Tod, das ist die kuhle Nacht • Handel/Angels, ever bright and fair • Ives/The Children's Hour and A Night Song • Lotti/Pur dicesti, o bocca bella • Massenet/Elegie • Persichetti/The Microbe • Scarlatti/Le Violette

Mezzo

ADVANCED LEVEL

MMO 9017
FAY KITTELSON, soloist
RICHARD FOSTER, pianist
Bach/Esurientes implevit bonis • Caccini/Amarilli, mia bella • Chausson/Les Papillons • Faure/Adieu and Après un Reve • Guion/At the Cry of the First Bird • Purcell/When I am laid in earth • Wolf/Fussreise

Contralto

BEGINNING LEVEL

MMO 9021
CARLINE RAY, soloist
BRUCE EBERLE, pianist
Brahms/Wiegenlied • Durante/Vergin, tutto amor • Franz/Es hat die Rose sich beklagt • Monteverdi/Lasciatemi morire! • Mozart/Die Alte • Scarlatti/Se Florindo è fedele • Spiritual/Ride On, King Jesus!

Tenor

BEGINNING LEVEL

MMO 9031
GEORGE SHIRLEY, tenor
WAYNE SANDERS, pianist
Handel/Ombra mai fu • McGill/Duna • Purcell/If music be the food of love • Scarlatti/Cara, cara e dolce • Schubert/Das Wandern • arr. Shirley/There Is A Balm In Gilead

INTERMEDIATE LEVEL

MMO 9034
GEORGE SHIRLEY, tenor
WAYNE SANDERS, pianist
Dello Joio/There is a lady sweet and kind • Leoncavallo/Mattinata • Massenet/Crepuscule • Mendelssohn/Be thou faithful unto death • Rachmaninoff/In The Silence • Swanson/Night Song

ADVANCED LEVEL

MMO 9037
GEORGE SHIRLEY, tenor
WAYNE SANDERS, pianist
Faure/Fleur Jetée • Handel/Every Valley • Scarlatti/Sono unite a tormentarmi • Schubert/Die Allmacht • Swanson/Joy • Verdi/Questa o quella

A new series by Music Minus One featuring performances by major American artists on the A side. You perform the same selections on the B side with the accompaniment provided.

Printed In Canada

MUSIC MINUS ONE • 43 West 61st Street • New York, N.Y. 10023